ANGELS ALONG THE JOURNEY

SUE MUELLER

Books Academy LLC
112 SW HK Dodgen Loop, Temple, Texas 76504
Hotline: (254) 800-1189

Ordering Information: Quantity sales. Special discounts are available on quantity purchases by corporations, associations, and others. For details, contact the publisher at the address above.

Printed in the United States of America.

ISBN:

Softcover: 978-1-968807-89-4

eBook: 978-1-968807-90-0

Library of Congress Control Number: 2026906396

TABLE OF CONTENTS

Prelude

Life is a journey. It is not always the road we planned. We can try to map out our future, but sometimes, God has other plans for us and takes us on a different trip from the one we intended. From the time we are born until the day we die, we are on a journey. But when you walk with faith, we are never alone. When we go with His plan, it works out better and more peaceful than if we go alone.

During our voyage, we sometimes meet people who travel with us as part of our journey, maybe for a lifetime, maybe just for an hour to two, or maybe just for a few seconds. As I look back over my life, I see many times God has sent me people (or Angels) that helped direct me, or hold my hand, or sit by my side for a time. I haven't always recognized that I needed help at that moment, but later, it occurs to me that it was just what I needed at that time.

God created Angels before He created humans. Angels are always Angels, and humans are always humans. When we die, we are still human. Hopefully, we become saints. But God has given us Angels to help us in our lives here on earth.

In His wisdom, God gave each of us a Guardian Angel to watch over us and help direct us. Sometimes, these Angels put in our hearts an urge to assist another person.

Chapter 1

I have found over the years that there have been times that some people enter my life to help me when I needed it. I may not have even known that I needed help. I have also seen times when I was there for someone who needed my help.

I believe that our Guardian Angels give us that nudge or inspiration to be of assistance to someone who needs help. We sometimes think of this as coincidence. But coincidence is God's way of staying silent.

People come and go in our lives – sometimes for a moment, sometimes for years. But there is a purpose for everything and a time for everything in its own time.

I went to babysit for my cousin, Carol that lived a little over an hour away. She and her husband needed an evening out. When they go back, it was about midnight, and I left to drive home. While I was driving, I hadn't realized I was speeding. A cop pulled me over and gave me a warning. That cop's warning made me slow down. Shortly up the road was some deer crossing the road. I would not have seen them in time if I had not slowed down because of that warning. I thanked God for that cop. (Angel? Yes!)

I think back when I met my husband. It was such a fleeting moment that we could have easily missed each other. As a counselor at a CYO day camp in New York, a bunch of us would get together and meet on Sunday at Rockaway Beach. There was guy who I knew from being a counselor, Mike. He saw Jim at Mass that morning. They never hung out together, but decided to go to the beach that day. Even though Mike was not part of our usual group, when I saw him on the boardwalk, I invited him to join us. I don't even think he knows that we got married. (Angel in disguise). I don't even know to this day if Mike ever knew we got married.

It was always our intention to travel whenever we could. Ji's mom always wanted to go places, but since we buried her on her fiftieth birthday, she never got to do much traveling. So we decided we were not going to wait to retire to go places. We started out to do it early in our marriage.

Jim and I have always liked to go places and see things. We started to travel on our honeymoon. One week in the Poconos at Honeymoon Haven, and another week traveling to Watkins Glen, Niagara Falls, Thousand Islands, Lake Champlain, Lake George, & Wakefield, MA. It was great to see so much in so short a time.

As kids came, we took them on many trips. We took two trips across country in a pop-up camper for five weeks each time. Once with three kids and the second time with four kids. By the time the fifth one arrived, we were in teen years, and they didn't want to go anymore. Besides, we outgrew the camper. We drove many trips to Orlando, Florida. We also visited family in Texas quite a few times.

It was always our intention to travel whenever we could. Jim's mom always wanted to go places, but died at age 50 before she could do much traveling. So, we knew we weren't going to wait to retire to go places. We started out to do it early in our marriage.

Our first trip to Europe was 9/9/99. It was my birthday, and we had to do something special for it. We went to Europe with my sister and brother-in-law. Visited Rome, Florence, Venice, Austria, Switzerland, France, and Spain. A whirlwind trip, but we saw so much in only two weeks' time. In Rome, we met an American couple that took us under their wing to see the Vatican. They had already been on a tour there and was back to linger through it again. So, we had a private tour through their experience. (Angles in disguise)

We have visited all fifty states. My husband always says we live in the 51st state – the state of confusion. So, it stands to reason I now run day trips, overnight trips, and cruises for our parish.

I had a neighbor whose backyard joined ours. They had a dog that was kept in a dog house that was closer to our house then theirs. Her teenage son would tease the dog, and once, I saw him pick up this big dog up by his four paws. I asked him not to hurt his dog. He ran down to his house, and his mother quickly defended her son and told me that he would never hurt their dog. Afterward, she would not speak to me. She turned away any time I would drive by.

She loved children, and all the kids in the neighborhood would always flock to her house, and she would tell them stories. I had to go past her house whenever I left, but every time I would go past her house, I would wave, and she would turn away and ignore me.

This went on for at least two to three years. Then one time, she was just turning around as I drove past and was caught off guard. She instinctively waved back to me. This was a game-changer. From then on, she would wave.

As the years went by, we would gradually talk a little. And after her husband died, we started to talk over the fence a little here and there. We eventually talked about God, and she would share how she would almost see her husband in the corner of their room. She felt his presence. I could see her faith increasing, and she started to go to church with her nephew.

Now living alone after her two sons got married, she was lonely. She stopped her newspaper delivery at one point. I knew that because my son, Jim, was er newspaper boy. She shared that she had cancer and was on a strict diet. I kept sending food down to her that I knew she could eat. When we went into the hospital, I visited with her and talked more and more about faith. We didn't share the same religion, but we did share the same God. She was very grateful.

I remember the last day I went to visit her. The bed was empty, and I just stood there. The nurse then told me she had passed away during the night. I felt so sad. But I was so glad that she had made her peace with me and with God. I thank God that I did have an effect on her. She had told me how my sharing of God got her to start going to church again.

I think back on this and realize that my Guardian Angel was inspiring me to reach out to her. I felt joy that I had this opportunity to help a soul reach her destination with God. This entire thing took many years, but in the end, God prevailed.

Chapter 4

Years ago, when we only had three kids, I broke my ankle. My very good friend Maryann, who also had three kids, would come over and help me and take care of fixing dinner for both our families. But when she scrubbed my kitchen floor on her hands and knees, I was so humbled. I didn't even do that. But I realize that she was the giver and I the receiver. The joy we get out of giving is so great. There has to be a receiver for those to give. In my way of being a receiver, I was giving her joy. I am more comfortable being a giver. It is hard for me to be a receiver.

Sometimes, we are the receivers, and sometimes, we are the givers. No man is an island, and we need each other to reach our ultimate goal, which is heaven.

On occasion, we travel alone. Like our cruise from Copenhagen to Boston. Our new friends helped us navigate our excursions so we didn't get lost. (Angels in disguise)

Our trip from New Jersey to Quebec was a bit of an experience when Jim fell on the ship and had to go to the Medical. He ended up with two black eyes. I even took a picture of him with a picture of some Racoons. Told him that was his new family. So glad he didn't get seriously injured. The medical team was great. (Angels in disguise)

He had some stomach issues on that trip, and the doctor gave him some medication to calm it down, and it worked. He took it easy, but we managed to finish the trip without any more incidents. (Angels)

When our doctor back home ordered tests, it showed he had lots of gallstones, but said it was nothing to be concerned about.

Chapter 5

Dave's Story

Our fifth and last child, Dave, was born on February 25, 1982. His closest sibling was Becky, who was three. Dawn was fourteen, Jim twelve, and Lance ten. He was raised with many "parents". He was a rebel from the start. Always debating and pushing the limits.

Not a great student. Since he had a high IQ, he didn't think it necessary to do homework. He learned everything in school by being there. He got by each year with us pushing him to do better. I even bribed him by telling him we would give him $1000 for graduating on time without summer school. Each year, he would pull his grades up the last minute. Every year, that is, except his junior year. He had to go to summer school, and he got by again without studying.

He had a car accident in March of his Senior year. Had a compound fracture in his leg, bruised sternum, and massive injuries to his mouth that kept him home for a while, and he didn't have the time to bring his grades up enough to graduate. He would have to repeat the whole year.

Dave's plan

He quit school without us knowing and took his equivalency test that Fall which gave him his H.S. Diploma since he did it in the same year. Again, no studying. Passed with a breeze. So he graduated with his class. He told me later that his late cousin, Tara, had encouraged him many times. I guess nothing we said mattered. I am very grateful to my niece for this.

Dave had many jobs. Not sure if I can remember them all. He was a newspaper carrier, as all our boys were. He worked at Dorney Park during the summers for a couple of years. At Giant Food Store, he worked until he took a snowy day off to go skiing and got fired because he couldn't produce a doctor's note. He worked at Weis Food Store after his accident, which he didn't like. Worked at a Valvoline Garage changing oil. A job at Spaghetti Factory, Yocco's Hot Dogs, a job delivering car parts to service stations, another at a construction site delivery, but mostly at Kirby selling vacuums. He did this for quite some time. He worked up to be a Trainer and really believed in his product. Even had his own office for a short time. Between his jobs at Kirby, he worked as a finance adviser at Wilmington Finance near Philly.

He got his insurance license and worked for Nationwide, but since he lost his driver's license, the company could not keep him. Worked at a Service Call company, Synchronous. That job went away when he decided to go back to school to become a nurse so he could better support his daughter.

Autumn was almost a year old when Dave found out about her. It was a one-night stand with a friend of a friend, but it produced this beautiful child. He loved kids, and I didn't want him getting involved before he had proof that she was his.

He had paternity test done before he met her. He was so proud to be a dad. Word spread fast. He met her, and he was in love with her immediately. He loved showing her off to everyone. He got her most every weekend. I believe that she made him look at the direction he was going and decided to make some plans for a secure future for them both.

While in nursing school, he worked full-time at Geico Insurance Company, where he worked until his death. Dave could sell anyone anything. If he believed in it, he could put up a good presentation. I often told him he should be a lawyer. He would debate his belief and make you think his way made sense.

He would always talk about his friend this or his other friend that. I said, no one has that many friends. Maybe a lot of acquaintances, but not that many close friends. He made a liar out of me. His friends that showed up at his funeral begged to differ.

One time, we were getting ready to take Autumn back home when his friend Daniel called to tell him that a mutual friend was threatening suicide and that he had guns in the house. Dave asked me if I would take Autumn home without him so he could go and talk with his friend. Daniel picked Dave up, and together they helped him.

Monday, February 18, 2013

I picked Dave up from work at 5 PM to take him to his class for nursing. Dave lost his license, and I was his ride. It gave us a lot of treasured time together. He loved to talk, and so I learned a lot of what was going on in his life. I felt very secure when he was with me. I never got lost. He knew shortcuts and roads that I never knew existed.

This particular evening, he said he didn't feel great and was skipping school that night. He wasn't a complainer, so I knew he really didn't feel good. Took his temperature, and it was ninety-nine. I said that was a good temp, and it was fighting off an infection in his body. He went to work the next day as usual. Said he was better, but then when I picked him up, it was the same thing. He wasn't feeling well.

Dave was working hard at putting his life together. He was almost 31 and was a little carefree until his daughter came into his life. Autumn gave him a desire to work harder to make a secure future for her.

Tuesday, February 19, 2013

After work, Dave had temperature of ninety-nine and didn't feel good enough to go to school again.

Wednesday, February 20, 2013

He had a day off and went to the casino with us on the bus trip I was running. Slept and studied on the bus. Had a good day at the casino and went to class that night. He had a test and said he felt good about it.

Thursday, February 21, 2013

He went to work and again didn't feel good that night – same temperature of ninety-nine.

Friday, February 22, 2013

He went to work on Friday and went bowling. Bowled his best game of 269.

Saturday, February 23, 2013

He went to work as usual. I didn't pick his daughter up for the weekend since he wasn't feeling well, and also, he had plans to go out for his birthday, which was on Monday. After work, he went to his room and slept. Not unusual for him, especially since his Xbox was in his room. Didn't see him again till Sunday.

Sunday, February 24, 2013

Told me he wanted to go to the doctor's. Since it was Sunday said I couldn't call till Monday, when the office would be open.

We left for a meeting in the early afternoon and mentioned to a friend there that he wanted me to pick up an inhaler. Janet said she had one and would drop it off. When she came, she was showing him how to use it and said she didn't like how he looked. She listened to his lungs and said I should take him to the emergency center. Since she was an emergency room nurse, I trusted her judgment and left immediately.

Stopped off at the urgent care a half block from the hospital, still thinking they would give him an antibiotic and send him home. When we got there, he walked into the waiting room but then told me that he would not be able to walk any further. I got a wheelchair, thinking this is crazy. After listening to his lungs, the doctor told me to take him to the hospital. In fact, they would call an ambulance. I said I would drive him the block myself. At the hospital, they took him back into a room immediately, and I called my husband, who was not home when we left, to tell him what was happening. I asked if he should come down, and I said "no", that I would be home soon. He told me later that he had a premonition that Dave was not coming home again. I was still thinking it is a bug that he needs an antibiotic for, and he'll be fine.

After mega doses of different antibiotics and still having his oxygen level at 92, they decided to intubate him. They had explained this before to us and said he would have to be knocked out for it. Dave nodded to me that it was okay, and I sat outside till it was done. I was thinking that they would then wake him. What was I thinking? I took a picture of him, thinking I was going to show him what he put me through.

He had told me not to call his siblings, but after they intubated him and knowing he would not be home for his birthday calls from them, I decided to let them all know.

The doctor came and told me they had him under control and were going to move him to a room shortly, and I should go home. It was 1 AM - his birthday.

I was informed later that Father Becker came in and anointed him.

I was awakened at 3:15 AM by a call from the doctor that Dave was not getting better, that he was getting worse. How could be happening? Jim & I were down in the hospital in 20 minutes. We held off notifying our kids till we could assess the situation. No sense in them losing sleep, too.

Doctor Singer (Chief Thoracic and Cardio) explained the lack of oxygen he was getting and wanted to use an ECO machine for him. It would oxygenate his blood, bypassing his lungs. Since he was unsteady, they wanted to do it bedside. We waited in the lounge area. At 4:30 AM, we heard CODE BLUE, room 2K11 – Dave's room. I fell to my knees. How could this be happening? Someone came out to explain things. He coded for 40 seconds, but now he was stable. They were bringing him to the OR to complete the procedure. It was then we called Dawn & Lance. Lance brought Jess & Dawn came over after she put her kids on the bus. Becky & Brad were visiting her brother, Jim, in Maine, and was flying back later that day. Jim decided to fly back with them.

After a few hours, Dr. Singer explained that "his visceral arteries were very small for a man his size". He called us into a private room and explained Dave may possibly need a heart transplant and that his only chance was to be taken to University of Penn Hospital in Philadelphia, and would be better that Penn sees him as their patient and not LVH's for this to happen. He was planning to take 12 hours off and go with him in the chopper. Univ. of Penn instead said they were sending their own team to pick up Dave.

I could not believe that what I thought bringing him in for an antibiotic turned into this nightmare. I was in shock. Jim & I decided to include our children in all the decision-making regarding their youngest brother.

We were told to go home and pack. Dawn drove us home since our kids did not want us to drive. Jess drove our car down to Philly. On the way home, Msgr. Wargo, our Pastor, called from the hospital, saying he was with Dave and anointed him. We explained we were going home to pack to be with him. He said they were getting him ready to fly down.

I packed and grabbed the Holy Water. When we got down at the hospital, we had to wait. I was very anxious. I should have been with him at LV Hospital until they flew him down. He was alone. I wanted to be with him.

Becky, Brad & Kyan were in Maine visiting Jim & Julie and were flying home on Monday. Jim decided to fly down with them. Becky & Jim met us at the hospital. Lance, Jess, and Dawn were also at the hospital. Kayla took train up from school.

Visiting hours were over at 8 PM, and we thought we had to leave. Before leaving the hospital, permission was given to hook Dave up to the dialysis he needs. We went to Becky & Brad's for the night. Jim stayed there too. Lance, Jess & Kayla went home.

The doctor called during the night to say they had to do a procedure to move the tubes in his legs, and the tip of a needle broke off. They needed permission to remove it. Gave permission. They called back to say the procedure went well.

So went Dave's 31st Birthday.

Tuesday, February 26, 2013

We all went to the hospital and took turns going in to stay with him. Dawn came with Meghan, Lance & Jess came with Kayla, and Austin. Dave's kidneys appeared to be working better overnight, so they did not put him on dialysis yet. By late morning, they explained that Dave needed more surgery.

Dr. Acker said that he would need surgery to take the tubes from his legs and place them directly into his chest. He felt the narrowness of the arteries, and the tubes in them could be contributing to the swelling and lack of circulation to his lower extremities. Also, he definitely needed dialysis, and they would put a tube in for that. Another procedure they would do is to make 4 slits in his right leg to remove the pressure that was building up to try and save that leg. He was already losing his left leg and both hands, which may be doing during the afternoon's procedures. They were not sure if he would make it through the surgery.

During the surgery, the nurse came in and said they identified the disease as Influenza B. When Dr. Acker came in while the surgery was still going on, he said that he was coming through it okay. I mentioned that the nurse said it was Influenza B, and he said he hadn't gotten that message. He just shook his head and looked down. He left to go back to the operating room. They never made the slits in his leg or put the dialysis tube in. They brought him back into his room. Shortly after, we were able to visit with him again. Everyone was so grateful that he made it through the surgery. Early that evening, we were making plans on who was going to stay where and what time we were going to be back in the morning. The nurse came in and advised that we were going to have a "very long night," and Dave would not make it through the night.

I called one of his friends, Daniel, and told him. 3 carloads of friends came down. Dawn called Mike, and Becky called Brad, and they both came. Heather Hillmann came and called her mom, Pat, and she came with Cheryl, Wil, and Brianna Scot.

We had holy water sprinkling very often and the rosary and Divine Mercy Chaplet being said.

We kept the machine going so his friends could visit him.

Dave died at 12:07 AM, Wednesday, February 27, 2013. He was surrounded by his parents, siblings, and their spouses.

The nurses cleaned him up and removed the tubes so we and his friends could visit with him one more time.

We left to come home and were numb. We were in disbelief of all that occurred. Got home about 4 AM, and Jim sent out an email to everyone. Called the funeral home and made plans to meet with him later to discuss the arrangements. We went to the 8:30 AM Mass and just prayed.

People came, and people left. We just went through the motions. Dawn, Jim, Lance & Becky came with us to the funeral home to help make the decisions. As I said before, all decisions were made together with our children. This was their brother, and they needed to take part in the planning. They even planned the eulogy after Mass together. They also picked the pictures at the funeral home for a slide presentation. Everyone needed to do something. It is part of the healing process.

Saturday, March 2, 2012

My sister, Judy, and her daughter, Dede, came. Heather brought Dave's daughter, Autumn. Maryann Cressman came and took Heather & Autumn to her house to stay. My nieces from Boston, Kathy, Tricia & Mo came down. My niece, Marie, from NY came in. We were fortunate that our friends, Kathy & Shyam, who lived around the corner, were on their winter vacation in Florida, and offered their home for our use. It was wonderful to have my family so close. In fact, they all stayed over an extra day so we could have some quality time together.

We had a celebration of Dave's life held at Rascal's, an entertainment place that had video games for the kids and had a backroom that we could come together to share memories of his life. We had a cake with a Philadelphia Eagle on it. It said "God Bless Dave," and an off-center halo was over the 'D' for Dave, who Autumn helped cut the cake. It was a good healing time for all.

Sunday, March 3, 2013

Jim's brother, Ed & Bea came and stayed over with us.

We had a closed casket since his body was pretty beaten up by all the swelling and could not be brought back to himself. We got there ½ hr. early, and people were already there. We stayed an extra hour, still greeting people. It was a massive crowd. Dave had many friends.

Monday, March 4, 2013

Mass was at 11:00 AM at St. Joseph the Worker with 7 Priests concelebrating. They were Msgr. Wargo, Msgr. Smith, Fr. Kevin Gualano, Fr. Joe Kweder, Msgr. John Martin, Msgr. Thomas Baddick, and Msgr. Yenushosky. We walked in with Autumn. The church was very full. I felt the love everyone had for us and for Dave. Judy & Julie gave the readings, and Dawn, Jim, Lance & Becky gave the eulogy for their brother. I was very proud of them, and their sharing was beautiful.

The reception was over at the Parish Center, and many people brought food. The Knights of Columbus and the Women's Guild help put it together and cleaned up. We were so grateful not to have to think about serving all those people.

Number 40 Significance in Bible 40-second preview with God, and approximately 40 hours later, Dave died. Lent evolved into a period of forty days in length is not surprising, as there are numerous biblical events that also involved forty days. Moses was on Mount Sinai receiving instructions from God for forty days (Exodus 24:18). Noah and his entourage were on the ark waiting for the rains to end for forty days and forty nights (Genesis 7:4). And Elijah "walked 40 days and 40 nights to the mountain of God, Horeb" (1Kings 19:8). Mostly, though, the forty days of Lent identifies with the time our Lord Jesus spent in the desert fasting, PRAYING, AND BEING TEMPTED BY THE DEVIL (Matthew 4:1-11). "By the solemn 40 days for Lent the Church unites herself with the earth year to the mystery of Jesus in the desert" (Catechism, no. 540).

Chapter 6

When Jim first mentioned this particular cruise to South America over Easter, I thought it sounded good. Our schedule was clear, and I said it might be like a little pilgrimage. A priest would be onboard and it would be a different experience to do the Triduum on a ship. Lots of time to spend with God.

Little did we know what kind of Pilgrimage God had planned for us. As a friend always says, "WANT TO MAKE GOD LAUGH? TELL HIM YOUR PLANS." Well, God was certainly getting a good laugh out of this one.

The day came to leave, and we drove into New York. The plan was to leave the car at Jim's brother's house and Uber over to the airport.

We last visited Ed at Christmas. He had been in bed for about 4 years. We have a full-time caretaker, Jessica (Angel), who was wonderful in taking care of him. She has been in this line of work for over 20 years. She had previously worked for Jim's cousin before her passing at age 94.

Two years prior, Ed's wife, Bea, had died. She had dementia and a stroke. She was paralyzed on one side. Jessica took care of both of them.

Jim had Power of Attorney for them. So, when Bea was taken to the hospital because her blood pressure dropped so low, the doctor called him and notified Jim of her death. He then called his brother to let him know his wife had died. Then called her sister, Betsy, in Albany to let her know. Betsy called back 5 minutes later to tell us her other sister, Louise, had died too. Wow! I guess Bea didn't want to go to heaven alone, so she grabbed her sister's hand and took her with her.

Driving into New York traffic was pretty heavy. It took us four hours to get to Ed's house. When we did, Jessica informed us that he had just taken a turn for the worse that morning. Hours before, she gave him a little something to drink, but he really didn't want anything to eat. She reminded him that we were coming soon.

We went into his room and saw that he was in a deep sleep. I spent a few minutes with him and left Jim to be alone with his brother. Jessica and I went into the kitchen to talk. I was planning to go back in to say the Divine Mercy Chaplet.

As Jim was finishing the rosary, he felt a presence of someone else in the room. No one was there, and when he ended the rosary, he told God that it was okay to take him. Two breaths later, he died. Jessica said in her over 20 years of experience, she never seen anyone die this quickly.

Jim's feeling this presence of someone in the room was a way of God comforting him. He had this same feeling of a presence before our son, Dave, died 11 years ago. At that time, he actually felt a hand on his shoulder that made him turn to look to see who it was. No one was there. (Dave's Angel)

We think Ed was just waiting till we got there. We were only there for 40 minutes. We arrived at 3:20 PM, and it was 4 PM. God has His timing. What a blessing for my husband to be with him when he passed.

It was a trillion/billion to one chance of this happening. We felt in awe. A peace that Jim was able to be with his brother and pray him over into God's hands. (A numbing and stunned peace)

We knew his death would happen someday and thought we would just get a phone call. Afterall we only went into New York a few times a year. But his was certainly a special blessing from God. (Thanking God)

We were in awe at God's timing. We would not have been there if we were not going on this cruise. Jim had the peace of being there with him. As shocking as this was, we were at peace. We knew this was going to happen sometime, but it is still a shock when it happens. Being there was such a blessing. God certainly has His plan and His timing. (Peace with Trusting in Him)

Jessica called 911, and the police and paramedics came. They called a doctor to determine the time of death. The Funeral home was called to come to collect the body. Things were going on around us. We were numb but needed to go through the motions.

Fortunately, Jessica was familiar with what to do. She took over for us as we made some phone calls. The next thing to do was to get us to the airport. Our timing was to Uber at 6 PM. We had a plane to catch. (Going through the motions and trusting in Him)

My mind was in a state of confusion. We were just going through things on autopilot. I was new at using Uber and was having a bit of a problem with it, but one of the officers helped me use it. (God providing and Angel)

We made it over to the airport, and as I was getting our luggage, I heard a voice from behind me say, "I'll get that."

Our son, Jim, was going to be our pilot to Buenos Aires and greeted us at the curb. This is one of his usual runs, and he planned it to be our pilot for this trip. What a treat after all what had just happened. God knew what we needed. (Trusting in His plan).

He already had our Boarding Passes and ushered us through the Airport. He took us to the crew lounge so we could talk awhile before the flight. We waited till we sat down to let him know about his uncle. He wasn't too surprised. He thought when he saw him the last time he visited, it was going to be his last. He saw how he was getting weaker. Since he flew out of JFK airport, he was able to visit him on occasion.

Before takeoff, we were invited to see the cockpit and meet the Captain. Then we settled into our seats for this 12-hour flight. Our son was doing the takeoff and landing. I felt very comfortable in his hands. (Also, in God's hands)

Chapter 7

In Buenos Aires, Jim took us to a Tango Show, Steak Dinner, and Palm Sunday Mass at the Pope's Cathedral. What a warm and peaceful trip. He had his friend and coworker, Laurin, who was a flight attendant on the next day's crew, look after us after he flew home.

We were still numb from Ed's passing. Our daughter, Dawn, was making plans for the funeral. Our son was getting paperwork done for the funeral home with papers that needed to be signed by my husband. (God cradling us with His protective hands)

Monday

In Buenos Aires, we took the hop-on hop-off bus and then had a wonderful and enjoyable evening with Laurin. Jim told us later that she wanted to adopt us. Our kids are negotiating a price. They were too funny.

<u>Tuesday</u> (Embarking Day)

We took an Uber over to the ship and all went smooth. Met a nice couple, Marvel & Keith from Utah, on the bus over to the ship. Had lunch with them onboard. We went to a specialty dinner that night. Just the two of us in the whole restaurant. Felt strange but very peaceful. (God providing)

Wednesday evening

We met our dinner companions for the cruise. Blaise and Ann Congeni. They were from Akron, Ohio. He was a retired children's infectious disease doctor that was giving lectures on the ship to other doctors for their recertifications. We enjoyed their company and lingered with them for a while after dinner. (Our Angel on the Ship) We went to the show that evening.

Holy Thursday morning

Jim woke with some pain in his upper belly. Wasn't sure what it was, but we were concerned about it being heart problems. He did have a pacemaker. We checked in with the Medical Team just to be sure. His EKG was good, BBP was high at 199/90, and his glucose was high at 298. But other than that, they couldn't find anything else. They gave him some medicine for indigestion and Tylenol. The pain subsided a bit, but he lost his appetite and energy.

The Mass of the Last Supper was scheduled for 5 PM. The priest, Fr. Murphy from NY, was sick on Holy Thursday, so Mass was cancelled. That was disappointing. Where is this Pilgrimage I was envisioning? (Trusting in God)

At dinner, Blaise was concerned with Jim but felt he did right by seeing the doctor.

Good Friday

Jim spent most of the day resting in our room. I picked up a bite for him from the Buffet for breakfast. No excursions, but he did go to dinner. Although he didn't eat much, Blaise was watching. (Trusting)

Holy Saturday

Jim was not doing too well. Spent the day resting and sleeping. He ate very little. Went to dinner and back to the room. He didn't have any energy either. Talked with Blaise, and he was keeping his eye on him. Jim went back to the room, and I went to the show alone. (Trusting in God)

Easter Sunday

The Priest was better for Easter Sunday. We had Mass, and the theater was full. Jim managed to get through Mass. Again, we spent the day in our room sleeping and resting. I went and got a bite to eat for breakfast and brought something back for Jim. He really didn't eat much. We went to dinner, but again he didn't eat much. His pain was not bad, but he didn't have any energy. (Thanking & Trusting)

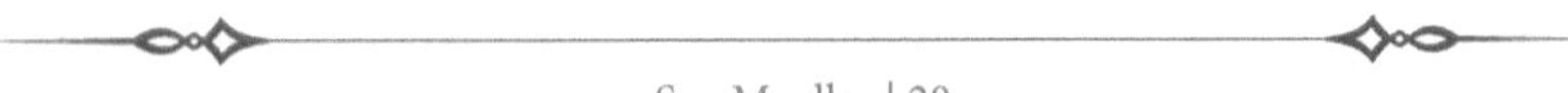

Monday

Jim's point of pain seems to be his gallbladder. Pain level was still low, but was more pointed to his gallbladder area. Spent much of the day in our room, but we went to the Sky Lounge and had a drink while sailing around Cape Horn. Didn't last long there and went back to our room.

We were just trying to hang on till we got to Santiago so we could fly home. (Hoping and Trusting)

Tuesday

Jim seemed a bit better. We went to the Buffet for Breakfast but Jim still didn't eat much. We still hung out in our room most of the day. Blaise was happy to see a little improvement in Jim. (Resting, Hoping, and Trusting)

Wednesday

We still stayed in our room most of the day. His pain was okay, but he was still very tired. Jim slept, and I prayed and watched TV. Went to dinner, and I went to the show alone. (Praying, and Trusting)

Thursday

I got some breakfast and brought a little bite for Jim. Still spent most of the day in our room resting. That evening, by the time we walked to the elevator, Jim had to rest. At this point, I got a wheelchair for him.

Before we went to dinner, I took Jim's temperature, and it was 99. When I told this to Blaise, he strongly suggested we visit the Medical Office again. He consulted with another doctor at the next table, who was a Cardiologist. He too recommended to go to the Medical Office. Blaise offered to go with us, which we gladly accepted. (So blessed to have this Angel)

When we got there, Jim's temperature was 102. The doctor immediately said we are disembarking. He was afraid he might go into sepsis. I was stunned and getting scared. (Trusting in God)

O God, where is your hand? I need to grab hold and have you pull me up from this crazy thing happening to us. You, O Lord, are in control, and I must let go of my control. You know how scared I am at this moment. I don't know what is going to happen. I turn to You to take our lives and surround us with Your peace, knowing You know all things and will turn this into good. (Trying to be Thankful In all Things)

I was numb. Where were we going? How were we getting there? What are their medical facilities like, and how are their doctors? We don't speak Spanish. We don't have their currency. We were just going around Cape Horn and sailing now by the Strait of Magellan. (Trusting in God and reaching for His hand)

We were alone. We were alone in a foreign land. We were alone and not knowing the language. Alone! So alone! Never felt this alone before. Feeling like I am in a dark room with no windows and no one to talk to, and not knowing where I am. (Trusting in God. I know He is with us.)

We were told I had 45 minutes to pack and get back down there. Two women came with me to our cabin to help me pack, and our cabin person came to help. I felt like I was being carried. Just going through the motions. Putting our lives in others' hands. (Trusting in God).

In our cabin, they worked really fast, and I was just grabbing things from where they were and putting them out so they could get them in the luggage. What a whirlwind. (Angels among us) (Trusting in God).

They took me down to the gangplank, where Jim was already there. They were waiting for a Pilot boat to pick us up. The waters were very rough and cold. It is very windy in this part of the world. Two guys, one on each side, helped Jim get from the ship onto the pilot boat. We had to step from the gangplank onto a wooden box, onto a tire, onto the boat. Then they took our luggage and then me. They were very serious and careful. They knew what they were doing. (Angels surrounding us)

All this is going so fast. My mind was not thinking. I was putting our lives in the hands of strangers. The doctor gave me a pill to take. I asked what it was for, and he said it was for motion sickness. I told him I don't get motion sickness, but he told me to put it in my pocket just in case. I didn't need it. (Trusting in God. Oh my God, I know you are here. Even if I do not see you, I trust in You). (Angels all around us)

It was about a 15-minute boat ride to the dock. A very, very long 15 minutes. The boat was definitely rocking, and the water was splashing crazily over the front of the boat. We got to the dock where they took Jim and put him in an ambulance. Again, they were very strong and careful with us. Our luggage and I were put into a car and followed the ambulance to the hospital. Another 15-minute ride. (More Angels surrounding us)

No one spoke English, so there was no communication with me. I had no clue as to where they were taking us. They could have been kidnapping us for all I know. My main focus was on what is happening to Jim. I did not like being separated from him. But these men were in charge, and I did what I was told. They had their instructions from the Ship and they knew what to do. (Scared but Trusting in God)

When we got to the hospital, they took him back to the ER. The hospital was a one-story building. The sign read Redsalud Magallanes Clinic. I sat with our luggage in the waiting room. Waiting! Waiting! Waiting! Time went by, and no one was coming to get me or tell me anything. (Waiting, praying, and trusting in God)

What felt like an hour, I finally used a translator application and asked the clerk when I can see him. The clerk checked in the back and then helped me with the luggage and took me back to where he was. It's a good thing we pack light. I was so glad to see him since I had not seen him since we left the ship. (Trusting in God).

They diagnosed him with severe gallbladder problems, and he needed to have surgery as soon as possible. They were ordering a room for him. Waiting again. (Trusting in God and Thanking Him).

Their app for translating was much easier than the one I was using, so I switched over to that one. Some of the nurses and doctors spoke some English. Hey were explaining things to me. I had to trust them with their knowledge. They were medical, and I was not. (Angels in disguise) (Trusting)

He was taken to his room later that evening, and surgery scheduled for 2 PM the next day. I slept in the recliner in his room. Not the best, but I was not leaving him. (Scared but trusting and thanking God for providing for us)

I sent texts to our kids. (They were now praying and trusting in God)

Friday

Time went by slowly. Surgery was scheduled for 2 PM. (Waiting & trusting. Prayer was our only friend now.

They finally took him and said after recovery time, he would be back in the room. I went to the cafeteria and got myself a sandwich. I needed something to eat. I really didn't have anything since dinner the night before.

So, I waited, trusted, and prayed. Surgery should only be an hour or so. (Waiting and trying to be Thankful)

Three hours later, they bring back an empty bed……. I sat there not moving….. No one to tell me anything……Scared to breathe …..(Waiting, Trusting, Waiting, Trusting, Praying, and trying to be Thankful)

Finally, the doctor came in and said that he was in the ICU. (I could breathe now)

She said she had to fight to get the gallbladder out, and there was a lot of infection and lots of stones. They put in a drain to remove the fluid. He would be in the ICU for 2 days with an IV for antibiotics. Even though it wasn't visiting hours in ICU, I went to check on him. He was groggy but okay. I reassured him. (Relieved but Trusting, Praying and Thanking God)

We requested a Priest and Fr. Marcus came and anointed him. He asked if we wanted Holy Communion, and we said yes. He said he would come the next day.

I slept in his bed in his room that night. Better than the recliner. (Thank you, God. Resting & Trusting)

Turns out Jim probably would never have made it home if they didn't make us disembark. They say it probably would have burst. Thanks to the urging of Blaise (our Angel), Jim is alive and going to be all right. We just wanted to get home, but Blaise assured us that what Jim needed was more immediate care. (Thankful and Trusting)

Saturday

I slipped into his room again. It wasn't visiting hours, but I needed to check on him. He was more alert and looking good. I reassured him. Waited for visiting hours and spent the time praying. I couldn't watch TV because it was all in Spanish. Definitely a pilgrimage. A different kind of pilgrimage then I was expecting. (Praying, Praying, Praying)

I went to the cafeteria only to find it is closed on the weekends. I ventured out across the street to a little store. I could recognize some things like yogurt, protein bar, a pound cake with chocolate chips, and some cookies. With everything in Spanish, I didn't know what most things were. Some things I knew I could survive on. It was definitely eating to survive. On occasion, we would get some good meals on this trip, but for now, I needed something nourishing. (Trusting)

I was on my pilgrimage. Not the one I was looking for, but the one God had planned for me. Fr. Marcus (another comforting Angel) came and gave us Holy Communion. Nothing to do but pray between the short visiting hours. (So Very Thankful)

Reassured the kids that their dad was doing well. Texted some friends and received many texts back. Knowing that so many friends were praying and thinking about us left me feeling surrounded by love. Our kids called to just hear our voices and know we were okay. (Praising and Thanking God)

Our daughter, Dawn, who had made the funeral arrangements for Ed, had to change those plans. She had already picked up some things from our house for us to wear for the funeral. Our original plan was to fly home on Wednesday, and we were having the funeral on Friday, but now that wasn't going to happen. After surgery, Jim couldn't fly for a week. So, she had yet another job to do: reschedule the funeral for Ed.

Our daughter Becky checked in with Ed's accountant to see what needed to be done with the estate. Our son Jim had the job of cancelling our flights home and waiting to see when we could fly home so he could make new flight plans.

Our kids were in charge of the funeral notice with a little input from us. They were working together to lighten the load for us. They were a great support team.

That night I slept in Jim's bed again. It was definitely better than the recliner, so I was getting some good sleep. (Sleeping and trusting)

Visiting hours in ICU were 12 to 1 pm and 3 to 5 pm. Very long days alone. (Praying and Trusting with more Praying and Trusting)

Spent much time texting and replying to texts. Grateful for those thoughts and prayers. I didn't feel so alone.

When I went to see him, he looked much better. Still not much of an appetite. I ate some of his food that he didn't want. Sleeping for the second night in his bed. God is good. (Thankful, Sleeping, and Trusting)

Divine Mercy Sunday

They brought him back to his room. We watched the Mass streamed from our Cathedral back home on the computer. What a week it was! His numbers were getting better. His BBP was good. Glucose 154. White count is coming down. He can't get up from the chair by himself yet, and his walking is slow, but he is walking unassisted. Pain makes you tired. So, he rested a lot.

I was back on the recliner for Sunday night. (So Thankful I could be with him)

Monday

They were releasing him. They untethered him from his IV and drain. Gave him a list of meds and diet restrictions. We made an appointment to come back on Thursday to have the stitches removed.

Our son-in-law Doug had a client whose mother-in-law lives in Chile, and suggested the Dreams Punta Arenas Hotel. What a nice hotel. It was like a resort. They had breakfast included, a swimming pool, a gym, a casino, a café, and a restaurant. Turns out it was right next to the dock where they brought us in a few days earlier. God is watching over us. (Amused at God's plan and Trusting).

Spent four nights there. Slept very well. (Sleeping and Praising).

When we checked into the hotel, we got a wheelchair for Jim. He still hadn't gotten a lot of strength yet. Even though they gave him PT twice a day in the hospital, his walking was still weak, but having the wheelchair worked very well.

At the hotel, they asked to see our Passports and immigration papers. We had gotten our Passports back from the ship when we disembarked, but they did not give us any immigration papers. Asked them at the hotel if we would need them to get home, and they suggested I check with the Immigration office, which was just across the street. How convenient. (God provides)

Tuesday

I went there the next day, and they helped us get our immigration papers. As I approached the very busy street, all the cars stopped. Wow! I guess they respect pedestrians. They were very helpful in the immigration office and gave me the papers we would need to leave Chile. (Angels making things easy)

We figured out how to make calls through the WiFi. Plans were starting to solidify. Our son could now make our flight plans for Friday.

Wednesday

Jim was getting stronger and walking using the wheelchair as a walker for balance. Had a nice dinner in the Hotel Restaurant.

Thursday

We went back to the hospital, and one of his nurses met us and escorted us around for his visit. He was our interpreter and guide. (Another angel) He was so kind. God is good. The stitches came out, and Jim was discharged. Yea! We turned in the wheelchair at the Hotel. Jim was now walking without assistance. (Thankful and Praising God)

The breakfast in the hotel was very good. The first day, we didn't make it there because our time was an hour behind theirs. We didn't know that. We found that out the day we left. I had put in a call to have our bags picked up at 7 AM on Friday. Fortunately, we were ready because they called at what I thought was 6 AM, but it was 7 AM. We might have missed our flight, or it would have been very tight. (God is Good)

We had made arrangements for wheelchairs for both of us. I can't walk or stand for that length of time, and pushing Jim and pulling the luggage was beyond what I could handle at this point. Our handlers were wonderful.

It worked out better than we thought. They knew where to take us and when.

Our first flight from Punta Arenas to Santiago was 3 ½ hours. In Santiago, we would have gotten lost. They pushed us from one building to the international terminal and knew how to get us through customs and to our correct gate. While waiting for our next flight, we had the rolls with jelly that I took from the breakfast buffet that morning. At least I thought ahead for this bite of food. (Trusting and God providing)

From Santiago to Buenos Aires was a 2-hour flight. The wheelchair people brought us to golfcart people, who brought us to the gate. The wheelchair people never came back to get us on board the plane, but I had a very nice gentleman help me put the luggage overhead. Jim was not allowed to lift anything for a month or so. (God providing again)

We had business class because the doctor said Jim had to lay down on the 12-hour flight to New York to prevent blood clots. (Trusting and God providing)

We did get some sleep and some good food on this flight. (Thankful for God providing)

Saturday

We arrived in New York at 7:15 am. We Ubered over to Ed's house to pick up our car and talk with Jessica, the caretaker, for a while. We stopped by the funeral home to pick up death certificates and then dropped them off for the lawyer. Met Jim's cousin, Bill and Faith for lunch. Time to share with family. (God providing)

We checked into the hotel and rested before going to Mass. Our kids wanted us to take a day to rest before driving back to Pennsylvania. We slept for ten hours. Felt refreshed for the ride back home. A rest we needed.

Sunday

The morning drive through Manhattan was wonderful. No traffic. What took us 4 hours when we first left, took us 2 ½ hrs. to get home. Our daughter, Dawn, and her husband, Doug, came and fixed us dinner that evening. So glad to be back home and with family. (Restful Peace)

Felt so good to sleep in our own bed. (Sleeping and Praising God)

Monday

Catch up day. Catch up on sleep. Catch up on wash. Catch up on emails. Catch up on mail. Catch up on phone calls. Catch up on paperwork. Catch up with God. (Thank you, Jesus)

Tuesday

Jim had a checkup with his Primary doctor. All is good. Just can't pick up anything more than 10 lbs. for a while. He should avoid too many fats. We had dinner over at friends and then we went to game night over at other friends. Felt the needed to be with people. (All of them are angels in our lives) (Thankful for the people God puts in our lives)

Wednesday

Jim is working through the paperwork for being Executor of his brother's estate. Talked with the lawyer and got things started. He talked with Finance company and got things started there, too.

Thursday

Jim is getting stronger and needs to get out for a walk. Had a haircut and strolled around Sam's Club.

Friday

Jim got some more paperwork done for his brother's estate. We had friends over for dinner before she started her cancer treatment. (Praying for her)

Saturday

Jim went to walk around a Landscaping nursery. He needs to get out for a walk.

Sunday

We rode back to New York for Jim's brother's funeral on Monday. Sunday is the best day traffic wise to drive into New York. Our son-in-law drove. Nice break not having to drive.

Chapter 8

Jim's Follow-Up

After being home a few weeks and getting through the funeral for Ed, Jim's healing process slowed down to a halt. All his progress was on pause. We had Mother's Day at our daughter's home in Delaware, and the next week, we went on a four-day bus trip to the Thousand Islands. But it was on Memorial Day that all changed. That week, Jim had a slight decline in his health. I was not sure if we could pinpoint anything particular but certainly was not on his upward trend.

Then on Monday, June 3, he had violent shaking for a half hour, and when I took his temperature, it was 102. I called the doctor's office, and they said to take him to the emergency room. They were waiting for us when we got there. They admitted him and took a CT scan, which showed a gallstone that was left behind and was blocking the duct, and the bile was backing up, and ulcers were forming. The infection was bad, and he was going into sepsis again.

Since he was on a blood thinner, they couldn't cut the stone out, so they did an ERCP procedure, and they inserted a sent. He was on massive ICs again. Blood cultures were drawn. He was finally cleared to go home on Thursday, June 6.

It was another close call. God was not finished with us yet. We still had more of a story to come.

For now, we had to wait for a procedure on July 12 to remove the stent and stone and a follow-up with another ERCP procedure, and afterward, the surgeon said they removed the stent, stone and some more sludge. The ulcers looked good. He does not need to have an endoscope when he had his colonoscopy. All looked wonderful.

That was until July 19 when Jim got a call from the surgeon's office saying they wanted a follow-up appointment on August 27. Now that left us scratching our heads. When he went for his office check for his colonoscopy on July 22, this doctor explained that he might want to wait for his coloscopy till after his next procedure.

What next procedure? Turns out there is a polyp.

During the ERCP procedure, they discovered a poly, and they did a biopsy, which turned out to be precancerous. They ordered another ERCP for September 18.

On September 18, Dr. Seng took out a lot of the precancer stuff and put in another stent. He explained that he could not get it all, but they would try again when they removed the stent set on October 21. If they couldn't get it all, then they would need to go in surgically to get the remainder.

In the meantime, he had his appointment on August 27 to get his quarterly pacemaker check. It turned out that it showed he had been in AFIB for a couple of weeks. Now we needed to schedule a heart ablation. That was scheduled for October 29.

My thought was that God was so good to us. If Jim had not had all these problems with his upper GI, we never would have discovered this precancer and been able to take care of this before it became a major problem.

Those plans were all changed when his surgeon, after the third ERCP procedure, said he needed to see an oncologist to discuss surgery. After meeting with Dr. Carr, she scheduled a Whipple surgery to remove all the precancer. That held off the heart ablation.

This was done on November 21. It was an eight-and-a-half-hour surgery. Jim didn't think he was going to survive. We had talked about it. He was at peace. So when I saw him after the surgery I recover, he was still groggy. I said, "Oho, you didn't expect to see me, did you? You expected to see him," I pointed to the heavens (God). "Sorry to disappoint you." We smiled.

He was in the hospital for ten days of recovery. He came home the Saturday after Thanksgiving. Sunday, our daughter Dawn brought over leftover Thanksgiving dinner.

The surgery revealed that there was an active cancer cell in the area of the stomach, but it was surrounded by precancer cells. It would have eventually led to stomach cancer, which would have been very hard to diagnose until it was very advanced.

Dr. Carr didn't think any further procedures need to be done, but she took it to the board of doctors, and they all agreed that no follow-up procedures necessary. The chance of catching this cancer early was nothing short of a miracle (Angels).

Recovery was going well. That was until December 19. He went into severe shaking. Calling the home care, they said to take him to the emergency. They were prepared for him at the hospital and admitted him. After many tests, they discovered he had a blood infection, not related to the surgery. They narrowed it down to a bad tooth. He had an abscess almost five years earlier.

The dentist at the time gave him three options: antibiotics, root canal, or pull it. He opted for the antibiotics. It turned out that it relieved the pain, but the infection remained. The infectious disease doctor, Dr. Le, was fantastic.

During that stay, they discovered he was having problems swallowing. They did a barium test and discovered that he had an osteophyte on his C3. It was like a bone spur on his spine. It sometimes caused him to cough to prevent food to go over the lung sidi stead of the esophagus side. It was probably irritated from all the anesthesia he had received over the past several procedures, which needed a follow-up with Neurologist.

After nine days, he was released with six weeks of IV antibiotics through a pic line. They set him up to go home, and the nurse arrived the next day to teach me how to do the IV.

I was amazed at the timing of everything that happened and knew that God was so very present in all of it. If he didn't have the gallbladder surgery, if the stone wasn't left behind, if they didn't do the ERCP's to get the stone out and then see the precancer, which led to finding the active cancer, it definitely would have shortened his life. So many people (and Angels) had a part in this and so many people's prayers. We are so blessed to have been part of God's amazing plan for our lives.

So not only was Thanksgiving in the hospital, so was Christmas.

What I learned and relearned

God is everywhere and He has the perfect plan.
We should not plan too stringently. Leave room to let God make changes.

God uses other people to guide us in His plan.

He uses us to get His message out to others.

God mingles it all together like stew to make a perfect plan for everyone.

He never leaves our side.

His love surrounds us and gives us strength when we do not know where the strength comes from.

He sends His angels to guide us and protect us.

Life is like a sailboat. It defers to the power of the wind. A sailor can maneuver when he cooperates with the wind. I can get through life's problems when I cooperate with God.

Many problems vanish instantly in the Light of God's Love. We are never alone.

Trust God in every detail of your life. Everything that happens fits into a pattern for good, to those who love Him.

Appreciate tough times because they amplify my awareness of God's Presence.

Be careful not to complain about anything, even the weather, since God is the Author of our circumstances. The best way to handle unwanted situations is to thank Him for them. This act of faith frees us from resentment and frees Him to work His ways into the situation, so that good emerges from it.

Quotes to ponder

"You are mine. Nothing can separate you from my love. "

"This is the day that I have made, Rejoice and be glad in it."

"Trusting Me is a moment-by-moment choice. Choose to trust Me in all circumstances."

"When I give you no special l guidance, stay where you are. Wait."

www.ingramcontent.com/pod-product-compliance
Lightning Source LLC
Chambersburg PA
CBHW022044050726
47591CB00003B/948
9781968807894